# Groupina and changing materials

Peter Riley and Dr Brian Knapp

# Curriculum Visions

## Science@School

### Teacher's Guide
There is a Teacher's Guide available to accompany this book.

### Dedicated Web Site
There is a wealth of supporting material including videos and activities available at the Professional Zone, part of our dedicated web site:

## www.CurriculumVisions.com

### The Professional Zone
is a subscription zone.

A CVP Book.
First published in 2008

Copyright © 2008 Earthscape

The rights of Peter Riley and Brian Knapp to be identified as the authors of this work have been asserted by them in accordance with the Copyright, Designs and Patents Act 1988.

**Authors**
Peter Riley, BSc, C Biol, MI Biol, PGCE, and Brian Knapp, BSc, PhD

**Senior Designer**
Adele Humphries, BA, PGCE

**Educational Consultant**
Jan Smith (former Deputy Head of Wellfield School, Burnley, Lancashire)

**Editor**
Gillian Gatehouse

**Designed and produced by**
EARTHSCAPE

**Printed in China by**
WKT Co., Ltd

**Curriculum Visions Science@School**
**Volume 2D Grouping and changing materials**
A CIP record for this book is available from the British Library.

ISBN: 978 1 86214 262 6

**Picture credits**
All pictures are from the Earthscape and ShutterStock collections.

This product is manufactured from sustainable managed forests. For every tree cut down at least one more is planted.

Butter melting in a frying pan

# Contents

|  | Page |
|---|---|
| 1: Materials | 4 |
| 2: Natural materials | 6 |
| 3: Metals and glass | 8 |
| 4: Plastic and paper | 10 |
| 5: Changing shape | 12 |
| 6: Heating materials | 14 |
| 7: Melting and freezing | 16 |
| 8: Cooling and warming | 18 |
| 9: Steam | 20 |
| 10: Words to learn | 22 |
| Index | 24 |

Weblink: www.curriculumvisions.com

# Materials

## A material is a substance which we use to make something with.

There are lots of different materials. Some are found naturally and some have to be made in factories. Words for materials include glass, sand, metal, stone, plastic, iron and flour. We use them to make everything from computers to concrete, light bulbs to cameras, and shoes to cakes.

The material we use to make this light bulb is glass.

The material we use to make the case for this camera is metal. The lens is made from glass.

cement    water    sand    gravel

The materials we use to make concrete are cement, water, sand and gravel.

The parts inside computers start out as sand.

The tops of these shoes are made from the material called leather. The bottoms are made from a plastic material. The laces are made from a cotton material.

The materials we use to make these cookies are flour, sugar, butter, chocolate, milk and eggs. Another name for materials mixed together is ingredients.

**Choose an object. Do you know what materials it is made from?**

# Natural materials

**The materials found in the world around us are called natural materials.**

We use stone for buildings and wood for furniture. We use wool and cotton for clothing. They don't need changing to make them useful. This is why they have been used for thousands of years.

Rock has been used to make many of the buildings in this ancient Middle Eastern town. The others have been made of simple brick – mud dried in the Sun.

The wooden frame and the cloth of this chair are made of natural materials.

Weblink: www.curriculumvisions.com

Wood and stone make buildings.

Shearing a sheep for its wool

Wool is made into clothes such as these socks.

Can you see any wood or wool around you? What is it used for?

Weblink: www.curriculumvisions.com

# Metals and glass

## Metals come from rocks.
## Glass is made from sand.

A rock containing a metal in useful amounts is called an ore. The ore is heated up in a factory until the metal flows out. The metal can then be made into useful things.

A copper coin.

Copper goes green if it is left out in the air. The famous Statue of Liberty in New York is made from 100 tonnes of copper.

This is copper ore. The copper is orange in colour.

The famous tower at Blackpool is made from over 25,000 tonnes of steel. The tram is also made of steel. The lampposts behind it are also made of steel.

This red material is iron ore. Iron ore is used to make steel.

Sand is mixed with other materials and heated. When they melt, they make glass. Molten glass can be shaped into useful things at a glassworks.

People have known how to blow glass into vases and other shapes for thousands of years. This is how it is done.

Glass teapot

glass blowing

**Can you see any metals and glass around you? What are they used for?**

Weblink: www.curriculumvisions.com

# Plastic and paper

Plastics and paper are two materials that have to be made in a factory.

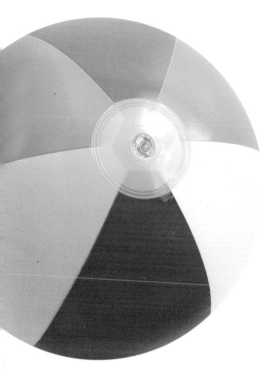

Plastic beach ball

Plastics are made from oil. Oil is a black treacly liquid made of many substances mixed together. The oil is boiled and the substances separated. The one that will become a plastic material is made into small chips.

The chips are taken to another factory where they are heated until they melt. Then they are stretched into sheets, made into blocks, pressed into the shape of bags, bottles, bins, traffic cones and many other useful things.

Plastic building blocks

Plastic traffic cone

Recycle bin with plastic bag and plastic bottles

Weblink: www.curriculumvisions.com

Wood can be used to make paper. First it is cut up into tiny pieces. Then it is put into a huge tub with hot water and the wood fibres separate out. The water also takes away the brown colour, and leaves the fibres white. The fibres are then pressed into sheets and dried.

The paper for books starts out on long rolls. Then it is printed, and finally cut up into pages and bound together.

Books begin as logs.

**Can you see any plastics and paper around you? What are they used for?**

Weblink: www.curriculumvisions.com

# Changing shape

## The shape of some materials can be changed easily.

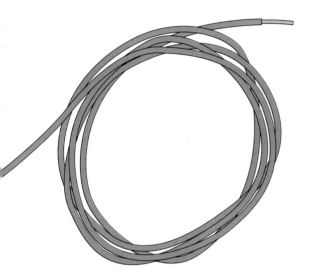

Materials are useful if we can change their shape. We can do this by cutting them, or filing. But it is very useful if we can change the shape of something just by pushing or pulling. Some metals, such as copper, bend easily.

Electrical cables bend easily. We say they are flexible. The metal they are made from is copper.

The steel wire used to make paperclips is harder to bend than the copper in a cable.

Weblink: www.curriculumvisions.com

Plasticine goes long and thin when you stretch it.

Clothes change shape as you move. They are made from lots of thin fibres.

Dough goes flat when you squash it.

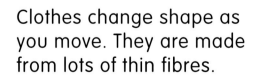

**What other materials can you easily change the shape of?**

Weblink: www.curriculumvisions.com

# Heating materials

## Many materials change when they are heated.

Fresh bread

Heating often causes a material to change into something new. Once it is heated we usually cannot change it back to what it was.

You can see what happens by watching bread change to toast. Pottery and bricks are common materials that change when they are heated.

Bread is a white, soft and bendy material when you take it from the packet. If you heat it in a toaster the bread changes. It becomes brown, hard and brittle. If you try to bend a slice of toast it breaks.

As you toast bread it becomes crisper on the outside.

Weblink: www.curriculumvisions.com

Clay is a soft material. Its shape can be changed easily on a potter's wheel.

Clay can be baked into useful things like mugs.

Baked clay is very hard and brittle and breaks easily.

Burnt bread is hard and brittle.

## What do you use baked clay objects for in your home?

Weblink: www.curriculumvisions.com

# 7 Melting and freezing

When something melts it changes from a solid to a liquid. When it *freezes* it changes from a liquid to a solid.

Ice and water are the same material. Ice is frozen water. Ice changes to water as the air warms up above freezing. Water changes to ice when the air cools below freezing.

These are icicles hanging from a roof. Icicles form when snow melts for a while and begins to drip from the roof. When it gets cold again, the water freezes as it drips.

Weblink: www.curriculumvisions.com

Ice can be made in a freezer.

Ice cubes melting

Snow is made of tiny ice crystals.

Snowflakes are tiny pieces of ice that have formed in clouds and then fallen to the ground.

Snow is a fluffy kind of ice. You can squash it together to make a snowman or snowballs.

When the weather warms, the snowman will melt, just like all other kinds of ice.

**What is ice made from?**

Weblink: www.curriculumvisions.com

# Cooling and warming

Some materials go soft when they are warmed up, and go hard when they cool down.

A few materials, such as ice, change suddenly from solid to liquid. But most materials change more gradually. As they become warm, they get soft. Finally, when they melt, they become runny.

Butter is soft when it is warm. It is hard when it is cold and will not spread on bread. If butter gets very warm, it melts and becomes runny.

A wax seal. Seals are made by melting red sealing wax with a flame. A ring, or some other object with markings on, is pressed into the wax while it is soft.

Softening can be useful or a nuisance. For example, it is useful to soften chocolate when making a cake. It is a nuisance to have soft chocolate when you are trying to eat a chocolate bar.

Chocolate is soft when it is warm. If you put it in the fridge it becomes hard. If you heat chocolate it melts.

A burning candle wick melts the wax. The wax flows down the sides of the candle. It cools as it flows and then sets hard again, making wax 'icicles'.

**Can you think of any materials that do not change when they are cooled or warmed?**

Weblink: www.curriculumvisions.com

# Steam

**When water gets very hot it boils and turns into steam.**

When you heat water very strongly bubbles form in the very hot water. They rise to the top and pop. We say that the water is boiling.

The bubbles are made of steam. When the bubbles pop the steam goes into the air. We cannot see steam. The steam cools down quickly in the air. This makes it change into tiny water drops. The water drops make the white clouds you can see near the spout of a kettle.

You can see the bubbles of steam in this boiling saucepan of water.

This is a boiling kettle.

Weblink: www.curriculumvisions.com

Steam is very powerful. It can make huge jets of water spurt up into the air in geysers. Steam is also powerful enough to drive steam engines, and to run power stations that make electricity.

This is a steam train. The train is pushed along using the pressure of steam in the boiler of the engine.

Natural jets of boiling water and steam spurt out of the ground to make natural fountains called geysers.

**Why should you be careful to keep out of the way of steam?**

# Words to learn

## Boiling

When water gets very hot and it bubbles and turns into steam.

## Brittle

Something that breaks easily when you try to bend it.

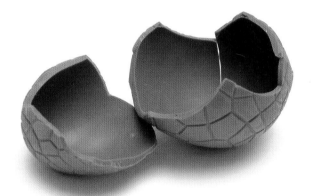

## Filing

Using a tool called a file to rub on metal or wood to wear it down.

## Melt

When a solid turns into a liquid because it is heated.

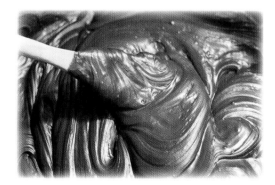

Weblink: www.curriculumvisions.com

# Oil

A natural liquid material made from tiny dead sea creatures.

# Ore

A rock that contains useful amounts of a metal such as iron or silver.

# Stones

Lumps of rock. They may be used for building walls.

# Pressure

A strong push. Steam pressure is used to turn wheels on a steam engine.

# Wax

A hard substance which feels slippery.

# Index

boil .............. **20, 22**

brick ............ **6–7**

brittle........... **15, 22**

concrete ........ **5**

factory .......... **4**

filing ............ **12, 22**

freeze ........... **16–17**

glass ............ **4, 9**

heating.......... **14**

ingredients ..... **5**

melt ............. **2, 16–17, 22**

metal ........... **4, 8, 12**

oil................ **10, 23**

ore .............. **9, 23**

paper ........... **11**

plastic .......... **5, 10**

plasticine....... **13**

pressure......... **23**

recycling........ **10**

sand............. **5, 9**

soften........... **18–19**

steam ........... **20–21**

stone............ **6–7, 23**

wax.............. **19, 23**

wood............ **7, 11**

wool............. **7**